I Like to Play

Dee White

Look at us!
We like to play.

It is fun to play
in all kinds of ways.

My name is Anton.
I like to play board games.

I play a game of chess with my friend.

My name is Poppy.
I like to play with my dog.

I do tricks with my dog.

My name is Jacob.
I like to play games
on my computer.

I play games with my friend, too.

My name is Kaylee.
I like to play in the snow.

I make star shapes in the snow.

My name is Harry.
I like to play with my plane.

I fly my plane with my sister.

My name is Lucy.
I like to play on
my guitar.

My grandma helps me play a song.

Index